A Patchworthy Apparel Book

by

Jean Wells

Illustrations by Marina Wood

Photographs by Vern Bartley

Garments photographed
made by Jean Wells unless
otherwise specified.

Welcome to "A Patchworthy Apparel Book,"
a collection of embellished design treats.

Yours Truly, Inc./Box 80218/Atlanta, Ga. 30366-0218 © 1981 Made and Printed in USA

About the Author

Jean Wells has been a stitcher since she was nine years old. A former economics teacher, she now teaches on a free lance basis at community colleges and quilt guilds. Yours Truly, Inc. published her first book, "New Beginnings in Quilted Jackets & Vests", in 1979. Jean's garment designs have appeared in Good Housekeeping Needlework magazine.

Jean is the owner of a very special fabric store, "The Stitchin' Post", in Sisters, Oregon. The store serves as home base for her ideas and inspiration. Jean is a people oriented person, much in demand as workshop instructor and lecturer on creative clothing ideas. She feels she is a teacher at heart, whether it's in her store, chairman of the local school board or lecturing to 400 people. Jean also enjoys gardening, reading, jogging, nature photography and family outings.

The Wells family, including husband Fred and children Jason and Valori, lives on eight acres ringed by snow-capped mountains in Sisters, a small 1880's style community near Bend.

JEAN WELLS

About the Illustrator

Marina Wood is Yours Truly, Inc.'s artist laureate and her illustrations are uniquely appropriate to the stitchery world. From tuckable teddies and patchwork rainbows to contemporary stitchery designs, she inspires us all to creativity. Marina and husband Bob moved to Lebanon, Oregon from Sisters, where she and Jean first discovered each other and the joy of combining their talents. The Woods have two children, 5-year-old Danya and Nicholas, 1½.

Reflections

When I teach a small class, we always begin with getting to know one another. In larger group presentations, I spend a few minutes introducing myself and I'd like to do that here.

On both sides of my family, I'm a fifth generation Oregonian. I'm proud of my pioneer ancestors I like to think I've inherited some of their drive independence. Both of my grandmothers were chers and quilters; my mother did embroidery. I an sewing doll clothes as a little girl. My mother ed some early projects, and I laugh when I look at skills — the techniques were certainly inventive! Iy interest in sewing and design continued to gon State University, where I majored in clothing textiles and spent one summer at Parsons School Design in New York. After graduation, I settled in teaching junior high Home Economics. It was a stant challenge to keep coming up with project as, but I wanted my students to have a positive, ductive experience.

Then my son Jason was born in 1969, I quit teach and vowed never to be a working mother. But, ut six months later, my husband Fred said, "You aren't the same person. Why don't you see about ng back to teaching?" To compromise my desire to a wife and mother and still have a small career, I ght half time. In 1974, my husband's urge to start own business moved us from Portland to Sisters, nall mountain community in central Oregon only miles from where I grew up. Fred is in the con ction business and does stained glass. Friends ed what I would do with two preschool children in the middle of nowhere. I knew something ld turn up.

started teaching patchwork in adult education. major obstacle, however, was a lack of suitable rics. So, with Fred's encouragement, I opened The tchin' Post in 1975. I had so much fun ordering se first fabrics, mixed with a terrible fear no one ld come on opening day. However, I quickly out w my store space and we built our own building t now houses my store and five others.

My classes brought enough local recognition that I was asked to teach a patchwork jacket and vest class at the first West Coast Quilter's Conference at Portland in 1978. There, I met Marti Michell of Yours Truly, Inc. She asked me to expand on the class and, in 1979, Yours Truly published "New Beginnings in Quilted Jackets & Vests." This book is an expanded version and replaces "Quilted Jackets & Vests."

While there is still emphasis on jackets and vests, I have included other garments, children's clothing, a great deal more on embellishments and lots of color pictures. Many words and some illustrations are repeated from the first book. I hope those who own the first book appreciate the necessity of the repetition.

This book was a great challenge. I wrote in the car, in bed at night when an idea hit, at my desk, in my sewing room. Often, I made a new garment to express an idea. My husband and children were encouraging and kept after me to finish. My son would yell, "Are you authoring, Mom?" before charging up the stairs to interrupt.

It was great fun to work with Marina Wood, who illustrated the first booklet. I met Marina when she was a customer in the store, carrying scraps of paper on which she'd drawn enchanting appliqué ideas. Marina seems to be able to interpret my words so effectively and adds excellent ideas of her own that inspire me in turn.

Working with photographer Vern Bartley opened a whole new world to me. Selecting settings, making all the final adjustments and finally checking through the camera to see what we had was very exciting. Vern is truly an artist with his camera.

The purpose of this book is to help you recognize your own design talents. Basically, I will approach embellishing commercially available patterns, not pattern construction. There is, of course, emphasis on my particular style and the methods I use. But, the primary goal is to inspire you!

Our delightful "Teddy" pops up here and there to remind you of important matters covered in the text. Teddy showed up unexpectedly for photo sessions and became one of the family. He perched on Marina's drawing board, giving her inspiration, and sat up with me through the nights, encouraging me to finish.

To me, the real challenge in sewing personalized clothing is to create something unique, universal and timeless. There is much time involved in this, so you must be sure your time is productive and your creative energy is well spent. There is a great sense of accomplishment to be found in a well done project.

There are limitations in clothing construction, but within those boundaries, there are choices and decisions to be made. I hope my experiences and suggestions will help you. I hope to help you set your own path, not give you step-by-step instructions for a specific concept. It is up to you to actually conceive the idea. If you find it difficult to begin, choose a photo or drawing of a garment that you like and start to reproduce it . . . in the process you will decide on a different color, modify the shape and, in the end, have a creation uniquely yours! The important thing is for you to be _involved_ in the creativity of the project. You may hit an obstacle, but don't let it stop you. Look at it as a mandate to look at other posibilities and go on.

Possibilities are myriad in personalized clothing. One thing leads to another. A simple fan shape is fun for a pinafore bib. . . then it occurs to you, "How would a fan look tucked into a strip pieced vest?" So, you try that. Then, you wonder about attaching several fans together into a border. There is just no end to the chain of possibilities.

Many people don't feel "artistic" unless they can draw or paint. Recently, though, textiles and fabrics have come into their own as a means of creative expression. By sharing my experiences and feelings, I hope to help you better understand the design principles that work for me. This book is a tool to help you start making patchwork clothing. Many books and patterns on the market tell you exactly what to do, but I won't. Rather, I offer you the impetus to proceed with _your own_ ideas. I hope these words and pictures open doors for you.

It was once the custom for friends to leave calling cards when they came to visit. Please regard this book as my card; it is a very personal extension of myself. It is my wish that it expand your world of stitching and bring you as much pleasure as it has given me.

Jean Wells

Getting Started

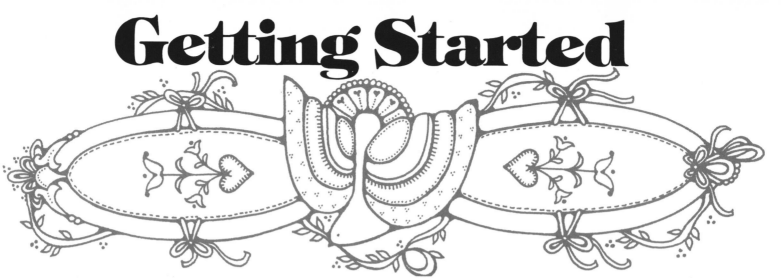

There's a vast difference between planning a design for a quilt and one for a patched and quilted garment. A quilt has four sides and lies or hangs on a flat surface. In contrast, a garment is put on a three-dimensional shape. Each person who wears a garment has a definite outline that must be taken into consideration. You may want to emphasize one part of that shape and minimize another. Keep in mind that you don't see the whole garment at once; you see only the front, or back, or side and front or back. The design must flow from front to back. The three-dimensional qualities of garments are what make them a challenge to me.

Remember that the neckline and armhole curves change the shape of the surface on which you are working. Many times, you may have to alter a design concept by lengthening or widening it to fit the space in which you are working. At first, I tried to use traditional quilt blocks on the back or fronts of a jacket, but found that many adjustments were needed. My experience is that I work better in the freer form of piecing. String or strip quilting lets me make decisions as I sew and allows the design to grow as I work.

Inspiration

"Open your eyes!" I had a college professor who began a basic design class with that challenge. I had no idea then what he meant, but, by the end of the semester, I had literally done just that. The world around us is full of designs adaptable to stitching. It's a matter of training yourself to see design possibilites in all things and to realize how they can be duplicated in sewing designs.

For example, lots of manhole covers have interesting designs, but most people never stop to look at them. We walk over them daily without stopping to note that they have texture and pattern as well as purpose.

You might keep a little notebook and, for a week, take note of objects that are circular or oval in shape; another time, note squares and rectangles. I like to observe design in unexpected places – a lemon cut crosswise has spokes radiating from the center; lengthwise, it has elongated ovals with circles (seeds) in a random arrangement.

What do these shapes, patterns and textures suggest to you? The pattern of the manhole cover might translate to a piecing design. The elongated oval of the lemon could make an interesting quilting design.

In the forest of the Northwest where I live, many people have wood stoves and fireplaces and I started taking pictures of their wood piles. Now, I'm not telling you to design a garment that looks like a wood pile. I noticed that each stack was different and that fascinating shapes were created in these individualistic structures. The shapes of the logs, combined with the shape of the stack and the swirling textures of the grain within the wood form a myriad of geometric and free form patterns. The ovals and rectangles within the structure interact to form designs within the structure. It is the relationship of the shapes and how they work together that can be translated into the design or embellishment of a garment. Take what you like about an interesting shape or relationship of shapes and let it influence your work.

The log cabin quilt block is famous for its strong diagonal division of light and dark fabrics. Visualize all the different ways of arranging multiples of log cabin blocks. Each woman who devises an arrangement has something unique she is trying to project. You can, too! Often, colors found together in nature will suggest a project. Jot down ideas as they come to you, wherever you may be. Let them rest and germinate in your mind and, someday, they may blossom into a great project!

Tools for Designing

It's difficult to know where to begin in planning a design for a patchwork garment. Sometimes I plan out all the steps on paper, then choose the fabrics. At other times, a particular fabric or trim will give me the idea of what to do. Be open to working either way or come up with your own procedure. I will point out all the things I can that will help you in this decision-making process. I will discuss several design principles that apply to clothing. Let them become tools to help you in your designing.

CENTER OF INTEREST – This is where the eye is first drawn. It might be a special pieced block framed with fabric, a butterfly appliqué, or a lace doily (see photo 24B). All other areas of the patchwork should be subordinate to the center of interest, which must be the most important part of the garment. It might be the border on a skirt or a bib on a pinafore. Don't put the center of interest at a place you don't want to emphasize (example: large hips). All other areas of piecing need to relate to the center of interest. If they should detract from it or compete with it, the garment becomes too busy. The vest shown in photo 17C is an example. The fan set to the right on the back of this vest is the center of interest. A lot of detailed stitching is worked on the back, but the fan is most important. The fan shape is carried out on the front with much less detail work.

BALANCE – This is the relationship of sizes, shapes and amounts of color. Think of a fireplace mantle; formal balance would mean that each side of the center is a mirror image of the other. The vest in photo 24D would be an example. Informal balance might be a candlestick on one side of the mantle and a flower arrangement on the other. Formal balance, or a mirror image, is easy to achieve. In informal, if you use a bright print on one side, use it on the other side, but not in the same place (photo 29A is an example). Amounts of color and shapes must balance from side to side. Using a small fan on just one side of a crazy quilt vest would not work as well as using one or two on the other side, too. The back of a garment is easier. You just work the design on the full surface and forget about the center. Squinting at my drawing or layout somehow helps me to tell if any part is too dominant.

REPETITION – The repeating of a shape, color, type of fabric, etc., is an important tool. While you are working, if a particular fabric next to another fabric really clicks, then do it again. The same goes for adjacent shapes. Repetition almost always ties the piecing together and gives continuity. Sometimes, repetition forms a pattern or some effect never suggested by an individual use of a motif or color.

COLOR – Nature has a such a wonderful way with color. Try to translate the colors you see in a sunset or a pansy into a garment. I have observed how nature uses similar tones together to create a feeling or mood. Sometimes, a sunset has subtle tones of dusty rose, mauve, slate blue. Other sunsets are hot pink, purple and red. Each has its own tone. I'm keenly aware of how nature treats amounts of color. A bright purple pansy with a small bright yellow center has disproportionate amounts of color that produce a whole flower. Translate that to a vest design with mostly purples and a small yellow accent. If mother nature does it, so can you!

Many times, a particular printed fabric will suggest the whole color plan for you to use. It's easy to work with something you've fallen in love with. Pin dots and other small monotone prints fill in nicely. Keep rearranging the fabrics until you arrive at a pleasing combination. I find it a good beginning to place together on a table fabrics that I feel will work in my design concept. Then I walk to the other side of the room and turn around. I know immediately if a fabric isn't doing its job. Sometimes one jumps out as unexpectedly dominant or sticks out like a sore thumb. Sometimes two fabrics are too similar and disappear into each other. If I get stuck on a project, I simply put it away for a while. It's surprising how a rearrangement or a substitution later can pull everything together. If the design seems bland, you can often perk it up by using a larger amount of your favorite color or fabric. You may have to choose another group of fabrics to work around the dominating one, or eliminate that color or print completely. But, generally, you can use that favorite fabric if you have the patience and imagination to find the right companions for it.

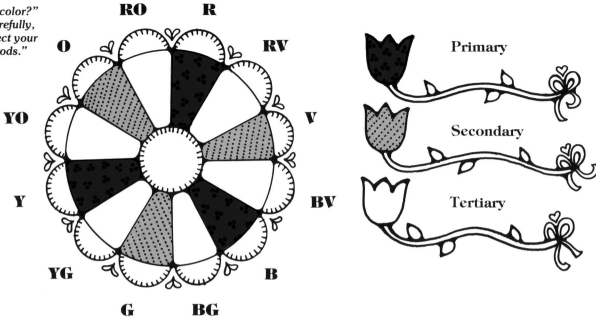

Primary

Secondary

Tertiary

The amount of color you use can establish or ruin a design. Equal amounts of all colors is not as interesting as using a large amount of one or two, medium amounts of most and just a touch of an accent color. Often, this accent is brighter or much darker than the other tones. The accent is the contrast or spark in the combination; it generally ties all the fabrics together and is necessary to provide interest. The little accent of yellow in our "pansy" vest adds life to an otherwise monochromatic piece.

Color is definitely a matter of individual choice. Color selections should reflect the personality and shape of the wearer. Most people start with a "theme" fabric. It suggests others that will harmonize with it. Try adding a color not shown in the predominant print, but one that is the same tone. This can be very effective.

You might try using all prints or all solids. The most difficult project I ever did was a red and white children's heart jacket (photo 36). I only wanted those two colors. I finally selected a solid red, red with tiny pindot, then red and white with equal amounts of each color, a white print with a small amount of red, and a white pique. By varying the amounts of red and white, I was able to achieve good contrast.

Let's take a look at the color wheel to help sort out the basics in planning color. It is organized the way nature uses them in a rainbow. Colors close to each other on the color wheel are usually the most comfortable to use together. Ones far apart have more contrast and take more toning down to be effective.

The **primary** colors are red, yellow and blue. They are called primary because all other colors are combinations of these. A **secondary** color is made from equal parts of two primaries. A **tertiary** color is made from a primary color and the secondary color next to it. Color wheels need not be complicated. It's a good way to familiarize yourself with the exciting array of color combinations.

Value and **intensity** are terms you hear when colors are discussed. Intensity is the dullness or brightness of a color. To change the intensity of a color, take colors opposite each other on the color wheel like orange and blue. Start with blue and keep adding small amounts of orange to it. It becomes duller and, when equal amounts are mixed together, you have a dull rust. A color is brightest in its natural state and dullest when an equal amount of its opposite is added to it. Value, on the other hand, is the lightness or darkness or a color. To change a color's value, add white or black to it.

Keep in mind that many times a color is brighter, duller, lighter or darker but still works in the overall color plan. I like changing the tones of pure colors in a color plan.

Intensity

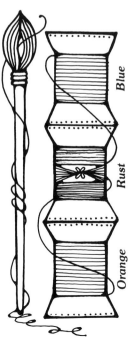

Value

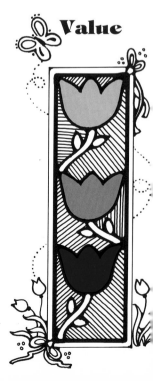

Color plans can be very helpful in designing a garment:

- ♥ one color plan (monochromatic) – shades and tints of one color;
- ♥ neighbors (analogous) – colors next to each other on the color wheel;
- ♥ opposites (complementary) – colors opposite each other on the color wheel;
- ♥ triad – three colors equal distance apart on the color wheel;
- ♥ theme fabric – sometimes you will discover a print that doesn't work in a preconceived color plan, so let that print dictate the other fabrics to you.

Remember, too, that color can be relative. The brightness of a particular fabric can vary drastically, depending on the colors of the fabric surrounding it. What you thought was a brilliant yellow may suddenly seem dull if you surround it with red and orange. Color is ultimately a very personal thing. What really matters is that you like it!

UNITY – When combination of color, balance, repetition and center of interest all work together, you have unity.

FABRIC SELECTION – In the color section, we discussed fabric colors. There are other important considerations. Fabric with a tight weave is easier to piece because it doesn't ravel. If you like a loosely woven fabric, try fusing lightweight interfacing to it before cutting. I like to use a variety of fabric textures to create interest. Let your tastes expand when piecing, try a new texture or color. You may eliminate some as you work. Not all preconceived plans work out. Preshrink fabrics you aren't sure about. You'd hate for a fabric to run or shrink after the garment is finished.

The texture of the fabric can definitely create interest in combination with prints. Imagine several blue and rust tiny cotton prints with a solid rust broadcloth. Then, consider making the solid rust a corduroy (with nap), a chintz (shiny), a rust and white pindot, or a grosgrain ribbon. Variety in texture adds interest and richness to a design.

COMMERCIAL PATTERNS – Pattern books are full of patterns that work for pieced clothing. Look for patterns with simple lines and narrow darts or no darts. Dresses with yokes are perfect. Look for lines that will allow you to add a pieced border. Patterns change constantly so it's best that you search through the books. I'm always looking out for places to embellish without being gaudy.

Buy your normal size pattern. The addition of lightweight quilt batting or soft padding for quilting doesn't usually demand a larger size pattern. My experience is that only when very heavy (5 oz. or more) quilt batting is used – as you might in some outerwear garments – do you need to consider a larger size.

Themes

In working with people, I find there are certain ideas we have in common and that they are comfortably applied to patchwork. I have chosen a variety of specific themes to discuss. I'll discuss how to use them in design, give variations and actual tips for construction. Some themes are harder to work with than others. Let this section be a place for you to absorb ideas or let one of my ideas inspire you. Sometimes, I get working with a particular theme and I just can't quit; I keep thinking of new ways to try it out. You will see an idea in its simplest form, as well as in an ornate form. Study the drawings and photos. Each has a message for you in terms of theme.

Grandmother's Fan

The Grandmother's Fan is a radiation form of design. The petal shapes originate from a central point. They remind me of the sun, the source of warmth, both physically and psychologically. If it's a sunny day, I'm just more cheerful. I like this shape because it can be varied and embellished easily. Take a look at photos 17C, 24D, 29C and 29E. I've made fans that are long and narrow, tall and thin, turned upside down and trimmed to pieces with laces and buttons. Round the outer edges like petals or make them pointed. Fans remind me of crazy quilts. I find crazy quilts so interesting because of the wealth of fabric, ribbons, trims and embroidery stitches.

Most of the time, strips of fabric are stitched together to form a fan and a quarter circle is added at the bottom. Templates can be drafted, if you wish. To draft the fan pieces, draw the finished size quarter circle you want, then fold it into the number of sections you want. Add seam allowances to the piece. Draw a small quarter circle for the fan center. It is sometimes easier to piece the fan and then appliqué it to the garment than to attempt to piece the fan into the garment.

Fan Fair

Photo 9A. Beverly Soasey is known for her landscape appliqués in a hoop. Here, she applied the same concept to a jacket. Beverly hand appliquéd all the pieces and some are slightly padded. Hand quilting emphasizes the shapes.

Photo 9B. String patch strips radiate from the heart of this vest. Piping between dot fabric and piecing outlines the shapes. Large prints like this gray one lend themselves to patchwork, adding dimension to the scale of the design.

Photo 9C. These are a few of Jean's favorite things.

Photo 9E. An old dresser scarf inspired the bib design for this voile pinafore. Embroidery stitches and grid quilting enhance the background.

Photo 9D. Marina Wood designed this apron for Jean Wells. It tells a story about Jean's sewing world in machine appliqué.

Everywhere Rainbows

Rainbows are probably liked best for their beautiful colors. I once saw a double rainbow after a rain . . . one was bright and the one above, subtle. That gave me all kinds of ideas. Rainbow colors don't necessarily have to be true, clear colors. They can be pastels or dusty colors. Think of all the color possibilities in a rainbow theme. In photo 25H, the pastel rainbow piping was responsible for the design of the jumper. This dress also shows that a rainbow doesn't have to make a complete half circle – it might make a quarter circle and hang from a cloud. Rainbows are more difficult to piece than most designs because they curve. The easiest way to execute a rainbow would be to fuse the pieces to the backing and machine appliqué. If you simplify the curve, it can be machine pieced. When I designed the rainbow jacket in photo 13C, I wanted the feeling of rainbows, hearts and sunshine (radiation). I didn't want to work with curves, so I used rainbow colors radiating from a central point, like a sunrise or a fan. The heart border balances the shapes above. Photo 25D shows rainbow colors used in a landscape type design.

Think of the rainbow theme in another way. Use the color ideas from a rainbow in your piecing. Look at the little blue pinafore in photo 36 that has heart shaped balloons, all in rainbow colors. The garment has a rainbow feeling even through it's not a rainbow shape. My daughter's log cabin quilt is rainbow pastels and has a very soft, "spring" feeling.

Heart to Heart

Hearts aren't just for Valentine's Day! Hearts are curvy, sexy, romantic little shapes that lend themselves to all kinds of arrangements. You can appliqué, string patch or stuff them. Let them dangle from a ribbon. My students practice machine and hand appliqué on a heart shape because of the curves. If you look closely, you will see many hearts in my designs. It's probably easiest to work with hearts like you would a trimming, as an added touch. (See photos 9B, 13C and 25D.) Gold ceramic heart shaped buttons inspired the design in photo 24D. I wanted to use the buttons as an embellishment rather than as a functional closing. To carry the heart idea from the back to the front, I appliquéd a border of heart shapes.

Play with heart shapes by marching them along together, reversing one and then the other. Then sketch quilting lines around them to see what happens in the background space. Or, trying working four, five or six hearts around a center point. It's almost a flower shape. Hearts can be a medallion in a block or work into a border design. Heart shapes are great quilting designs, too.

og Cabin

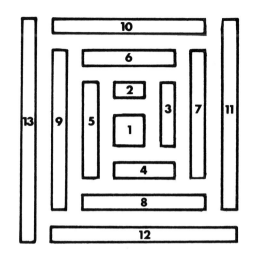

Log Cabin is probably one of the oldest forms of patchwork. Its many variations can be mind boggling. It's a design men relate to easily. Maybe they can visualize the log home being built on each block. I used to look at log cabin blocks and wonder and wonder how they were put together. I kept trying to work from the outside in. When it finally dawned on me to start at the center and work out, it was so simple that I felt like a complete fool.

Most log cabin blocks consist of light and dark strips, either arranged next to each other or opposite each other. Lights placed opposite each other create a V shape called Courthouse eps. When lights are adjacent, the block forms a diagonal. Traditionally, the center square was red to represent e fireplace or heart of the home.

For Christmas one year, I wanted to work in subtle reds and greens so the children would be comfortable wearing e garments later in the year. Using deep, burgandy red for the center, I worked outward with a diagonal form of log bin. (See photos 12E and 25G.) Jason's shirt yoke uses one block on each side of the front. A roof over a single ock makes a house shape pinafore bib with a button for the door knob. By putting several blocks together, a border as created on the bottom of the skirt. The basket lid was an experiment in minature (¼" wide strips) piecing.

I've found that by applying the stripping technique in log cabin piecing, you can solve all kinds of problems of fill-g space on garments. Many times a medallion shape on a jacket is finished off with log cabin type piecing. I've even ne so far as to try piecing ¼" strips to make minature blocks. You can see this in my son's shirt shown in photo 2F. I find I get the best results when I use all the same weight fabrics. Heavier fabrics or ones with nap take up ore space because of their added weight or fullness.

Log cabin has many uses in patchwork garments. One block might be a medallion on a vest or the yoke front on a irt or dress (photo 12C). Several blocks formed into a border might line the bottom edge of a skirt, or come down e front of a jacket. To make the border shown in photo 12D, I string patched the center block and just pieced on o sides of the center. It's really only half of the log cabin block. You might piece a whole jacket in log cabin, like a uilt. I used one block with a "roof" for the bib of my daughter's pinafore. How about a whole town of houses using log bin blocks? You can always add more strips on one side to create a contemporary house. The ultimate design ight be creating a landscape scene, using log cabin blocks, on a jacket.

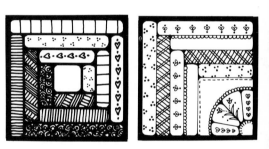

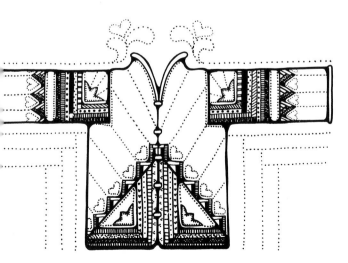

To actually piece a log cabin block, I find the following instructions to be most helpful. There are many ways to approach this project.

- Decide on the width you'd like the finished strips to be. Add ¼" seam allowances.
- Choose three or four light colors and three or four dark colors. The number depends on how large you want the blocks to be.
- Choose a solid for the center square.
- If the center block is 1½" square, it will be 1" square finished. The other strips should be cut 1½" wide to finish to 1".
- Place a light strip on the center square, right sides together. Stitch a ¼" seam, then trim strip even with center square.
- Make one turn with the block and add a second light strip, sewing through the first strip and center block.
- Add a dark strip to the next side. Continue until the block is the size you want.
- If finger pressing is insufficient, press the block with an iron after stitching each strip.

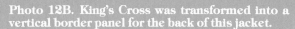

Photo 12A. Miniature (¼") strips make a log cabin yoke on Jason's shirt. The kitty ceramic buttons inspired Valori's simple string patch vest that can be worked with jeans as well as this pretty dress.

Photo 12D. Marina Wood drew this design as an address label for Jean, who made it a vest. It has many of Jean's favorite things: mountains, baskets, hearts, log cabin and string piecing.

Photo 12E. This shirt shows single log cabin blocks used as yoke sections. The pinafore bib is a single block with a rooftop and a button doorknob. Joined blocks form a matching border for the apron hem.

Photo 12C. The solid colors and a variety of texture in the log cabin yoke complement print fabric of Cindy Summerfield's dress. ing separates the yoke from the dress fabric

Photo 12F. An Amish log cabin quilt inspir the design and colors of this shirt yoke. T finished width of the strips is ⅜".

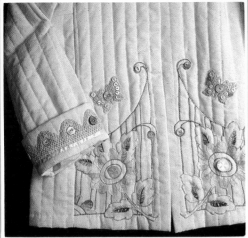
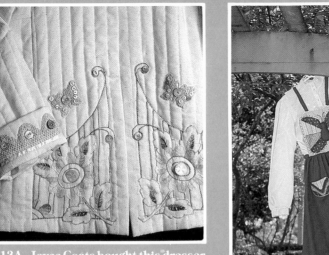

Photo 13A. Joyce Coats bought this dresser scarf at a flea market, appliquéd it to a pre-quilted background and then embellished it with buttons from her private collection.

Photo 13D. "A Pat on the Back" vest by Sally Paul showns an imaginative use of an old lace glove as the focal point of a medallion design.

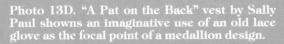

Photo 13C. "Rainbow Heartbeat" was created with Creative Cut-ups (Page 22). Machine quilting creates a durable sculptured look in children's clothing.

Photo 13E. Sally Paul cut string patchwork into strips to create an interesting effect on this jacket front and sleeves.

Levels of Involvement

After thinking about design ideas and fabrics, you should consider how to execute the project. Ask yourself these questions: How much time can I spend on it? . . . Who will be wearing it? . . . What kind of use will the garment receive? . . . What sewing technique will best carry out my idea? A child's coat or vest will probably get a lot of wear and tear, so machine stitching will be most durable. An evening jacket for special occasions will not receive as much wear, so more fragile techniques might be explored here. All the garments I make are machine washable. Many people think because a garment is pieced and pretty, it isn't washable. If properly constructed of washable fabrics, there is no reason not to machine wash your patchwork.

In this section, think about each technique described. I have simplified them as much as possible. Try to see how a design can be carried out in a variety of ways, each of which offers a different effect.

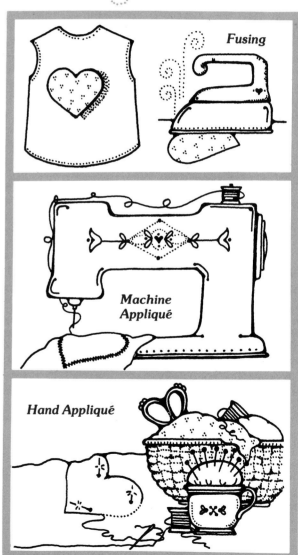

FUSING – In my college home economics sewing classes, fusing was a dirty word. In the years since, fusible products have improved greatly, along with our ideas for using them. You will need a fusible web to place between two fabrics. Each interfacing company has its own brand name. They all work well if you follow the directions given. Basically, you would cut a heart shape out of webbing, the same as your fabric shape. Place the web on the background fabric, with the fabric shape on top of the web. Be sure all webbing is under the fabric. Now, place the iron flat on the shape, count to 10, and lift the iron straight up. If you move the iron around before there is a good fuse, you may wrinkle the fabric. No stitching is required around the edges if the web is cut to come right to the edge of the shape. I often machine zigzag the edges anyway.

MACHINE APPLIQUÉ – Yours Truly, Inc. has an excellent book on machine appliqué that goes into much detail. My explanation will be very simple.

Cut out the shapes to be appliquéd. If the fabric is lightweight, you may want to put fusible interfacing behind it, or you could fuse the shape to the background fabric. Also, there is a product now available to home sewers called "tear away stabiizer". It looks like interfacing and it is placed under the background fabric to hold the fabric in place while you sew. Then you just tear it away.

Set the width of the stitch to wide and the number of stitches per inch close together (about 20 stitches per inch). Let the fabric feed through the machine at its own speed for the most consistent stitches. Sometimes, I go over a design a second time to make it look more satiny (cotton thread fills in better than polyester thread). You may choose to set the zigzag far apart the first time, then go over it a second time with a closer stitch. This is a very durable form of decorative work. Marina Wood designed the appliqués on the long apron in photo 9D. Many of the shapes are small, but can be machine appliquéd. The skirt in photo 36 shows how two heart shapes have been machine appliquéd together, then attached to the skirt waistband.

HAND APPLIQUÉ – Hand appliqué gives the shape a more sculptured look. It is more fragile and less durable than machine stitching. Some different hand stitches are illustrated in Back to Basics.

Transparent Appliqué

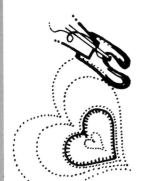

Machine Quilting

Hand Quilting

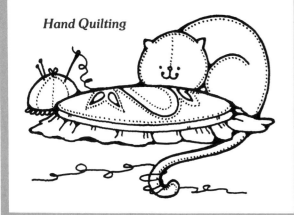

Free Form Padded Shapes

Cut the shapes ⅛" to ¼" larger all around than the desired finished shape. Where one piece must tuck under another, allow ½" on that edge. You can pin shapes in place or hand baste them if there are a lot. Let your fingers fold under the seam allowance as you go. Don't try to have all the edges turned or pressed under before you begin – you'll just become frustrated. Small stitches will hold the pieces in place best.

Patchwork designs like clamshell may be done by hand (photo 25B). The landscape jacket shown in photo 9A was hand appliquéd by Beverly Soasey. You may choose to pad some shapes as you go.

TRANSPARENT APPLIQUÉ – Transparent appliqué is the technique in which a voile, organdy or other "see-through" fabric is placed over an appliqué and held in place with quilting or embroidery stitches. The stitches add character and detail to the design.

Felt can be used under the voile, but it's not as washable as woven fabric. Also, I have found that bright colors work better than dark ones. The voile tones down the color and a dark color can look muddy under it. The shape can be fused in place, zigzagged or hand appliquéd before the voile is added. On the pinafore in photo 33F, the fused hearts were a hot pink pindot, but they appear pastel with ecru work overlay. There is no extra padding under the hearts, but they appear sculptured because of the hand stitching around each one.

MACHINE QUILTING – Baste the top layer, padding and backing together. If it is a small space, pins can hold the layers in place. Set your machine at 10-12 stitches to the inch. Machine stitch ¼" from the stitching or sew right in the seam (stitch in the ditch). Pay close attention to the lining or backing; sometimes it will pucker because of the loft of the batting. I like to place each of my hands out flat on each side of the presser foot and lightly guide the fabric. When finished with a section, pull the top thread to the back, tie a secure knot and clip off the tails. Start each section at the same end of the garment since the lining will move as you stitch. The vest in photo 9B was machine quilted.

HAND QUILTING – There are different approaches to hand quilting, an enjoyable and time honored craft that does wonderful things for garments.

Baste the three layers together, the same as for machine quilting. If necessary, lightly mark quilting lines with washable marking pens, soap or some other method you like. I use quilting thread because it is strong and doesn't tangle. A hoop or small frame is optional to hold your project taut. Knot a single thread, about 12" to 18" long. Quilting needles are very sharp and travel more easily through the fabrics than standard sewing needles. A thimble is helpful. The needle should travel straight through the fabric and batting, catch the lining, and come up as straight as possible. The thickness of your padding is a big factor in the length of your stitches. Try to get three or four stitches on the needle, then push the needle with the thimble finger through the fabric. The stitches can be placed parallel to a seam or you may want to quilt a design in a blank space.

Try to expand your ideas about quilting. Look at the clamshell vest in photo 25B. The quilting is varied, instead of continuing to follow the shape of the clamshells. I sometimes let the shape become taller, wider or longer. By varying these shapes, the quilting becomes much more interesting.

FREE FORM PADDED SHAPES – Especially on children's things, I like to see simple shapes filled with padding snapped on a pocket or dangling from a ribbon. The pinafore in photo 36A has hanging hearts. My 7-year-old wore it for a year before the photo was taken, so it does wash and wear. The shape is cut out and stitched like a pillow, and stuffed fairly tightly with polyester filling. Hand stitch shut the opening and attach the shape to the garment.

Embellishments

Laces — "Old & New"

My grandmothers and Jean Ray Laury (author of "New Uses for Old Laces") opened my mind to laces. Both my grandmothers did handwork, and I was blessed with a hope chest when I married. My mother used to embroider to relax in the evenings. Growing up with all this must have really sunk in because I've always loved laces, old quilts and embroidery. My inherited pieces remained in the cedar chest until I saw Jean's book. She encouraged me to use these old pieces. I started with pillows and wall pieces and now I love using them in garments. Jean's book goes into detail about laces and is an excellent reference. I will discuss their use on garments only.

The sentimental value of inherited lace will determine its use. Some pieces I really treasure are used on a dresser or framed. Once lace is put on a garment, it will get worn. It can be retrieved when you are tired of the garment. Usually, I use purchased lace in a garment rather than sentimental ones. It's still hard for me to cut into a doily. I can cut off a piece of pillowcase edging or, if a piece is frayed or in need of repair, I can cut it easily. I almost feel justified in making use of it!

It is wise to know about the care of laces. Laces are often discovered in old attic trunks, at flea markets, yards sales or antique stores. Because you are unaware of their history, examine them carefully. If they need cleaning, wash gently in warm sudsy water, rinse thoroughly and dry on a towel. If there are stubborn stains, lemon juice is excellent for bleaching and some people then spread them on green grass in the sun to dry. Hydrogen peroxide diluted to a weak solution also works. A strong bleach will weaken threads. When all else fails, sometimes dry cleaning works. If the lace is white and a stain persists, you can dye the lace with coffee or tea. I test my coffee or tea with 100% cotton fabric before putting the lace in. Commercial fabric dyes work, too. Heat will set a stain, so don't press the lace until it's the way you want it. Some laces will need starch to perk them up.

To begin using lace in a garment, spread out your choices and study them. Will the lace be the focal point? . . . Should it combine with piecing to create the focal point? . . . Will it embellish a pieced design?

The types of laces you work with help make decisions for you. Damaged or short pieces work well into pieced designs. Their edges usually are frayed and must be covered with ribbon, fabric or other lace. A reverse appliqué technique (discussed in Back to Basics) is a good possibility. Landscape settings lend themselves to cut up pieces – lace can appear as a field, a snow capped mountain, an old house or a tree. Let the lace speak for itself. Squint and look at the lace, relax and see what it says to you. Pillowcase edgings work for a border or an insert in strip piecing (photo 17B). Small pieces can be worked into crazy patch or string patch (photo 29A). I save even the finest pieces for this purpose. Parts of old tablecloths work here, too.

If you have a very pretty doily (circular, oval, square, rectangular) in good condition, consider making it a medallion. The ecru and white jacket in photo 24B was designed this way. I found the doily at an old store at the beach. It was mine for 88¢! I know I'll never have a find like that again. Sally Paul let a

Photo 17A. Dresser scarves can be used effectively as yokes or medallions in vest designs. Dori Williams cut apart this heart shaped lace border to set it in a vertical row down the back of this vest.

Photo 17B. The black print inspired Jean's choice of fabrics for this vest, decorated with family laces and doilies to highlight the crazy string patch design. Ribbons run through the lace eyelets to further decorate the designs.

Photo 17C. Crazy string patch is used in this design (see page 31). The simple shapes [li]ke to embellishment with lace, ribbons and buttons. The closeup shows ribbons [att]ached with embroidery stitches (see Page 19). The quilting illustrates a more con[tem]porary approach to hand quilting.

Photo 17D. The fan motif is the center of interest on the back of this jacket. Set slightly above center for better balance, it is enhanced by buttons, laces and string patching below.

lace glove become the focal point of her vest, shown in photo 13D. Once you have a design idea, you can start selecting fabrics. Don't have your mind completely made up because you may discover something else that works better once you begin.

The background fabric is extremely important. Consider texture and color in relationship to the lace and the design. Usually a firmly woven, heavier fabric is desirable because of the weight of the lace. If more stability is needed, you can use a thin batting or needlepunch behind the fabric. Since the lace is an important part of the design, choose a color of fabric to enhance the lace. A dark fabric gives contrast and distinction to white or ecru lace while a lighter fabric gives a softer, gentler feeling. What feeling do you want to create? The ecru jacket is very monochromatic, subtle and soft while some of the other lace pieces pictured show the lace off to a greater degree because of a darker fabric behind them. Do be careful with a print behind a lace. The shapes in the print sometimes fight with the detail of the lace. If I use a print, I choose a two color muted one rather than a busy one. Remember, the lace is adding another dimension to your composition – texture. The mere fact it's made of coarser threads makes it stand out. Once the background fabric is chosen, the other fabric choices should enhance your selection, not detract from it. If there is too much difference between the doily part and the other piecing, it will act as a "bullseye."

To attach lace by hand, use matching thread and tiny, close together stitches. Because the lace will be worn, it has a tendency to droop if it isn't attached securely. You can machine stitch it in place, too. On doilies, you will need several rows of stitching so the center is also attached. Edgings can be inserted in a seam in strip piecing. Or, you can place them on a strip and attach by hand. When further strip piecing is done, the raw edges of the outer ends will be covered.

Further embellishment with embroidery stitches will emphasize or repeat the shapes on the edges of the doilies or edgings (photo 29E). In Back to Basics, a glossary of embroidery stitches is illustrated. Several garments show how embroidery carries the theme out even further. (See photos 17C and 29A.) I use tiny ribbons and pull them through the laces, tie little bows and add buttons.

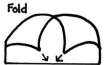

uttons

My husband constantly teases me that I never get buttons sewn on his shirts but am constantly decorating garments with buttons. I guess it's just more fun to have buttons work for you in a design than to mend. For my birthday several years ago, a close friend gave me an old canning jar full of white pearl buttons she had found at an antique sale. The buttons sat with my doilies from the beach and my mirage of fabric for a couple of months. Then, one day, it clicked and I did the ecru and white jacket (photo 24B). That was my first button experience. I discovered that the back side of a pearl button is often more interesting than the front.

There aren't a lot of rules about using buttons except to stitch them down securely. Tie knots in your thread after each button on the back side. It's an awful feeling to start losing buttons as you wear the garment.

Buttons can almost become a focal point of the garment, as in the teal a[nd] brown modified fan jacket (photo 29E). The jacket is actually weighed do[wn] from all the buttons along the bottom of the fans. The buttons are overlapp[ed] to achieve more height. Several varieties of buttons were used on this pie[ce.] Because I use lots of buttons, I buy up jars of them in antique or junk stor[es.] You can purchase antique buttons one at a time, but I find them too cos[tly] when I use lots. On the plum dresden vest (photo 24D), gold glazed ceram[ic] heart buttons decorate the petal shape pieces. I designed the vest around t[he] heart shaped buttons. On the rose jacket with pieced border shown in ph[oto] 25A, you'll find interesting, one-of-a-kind buttons tucked in special plac[es.] Cat buttons dominate the front of the vest shown in photo 12A.

♥ Buttons can help to repeat or emphasize a shape.
♥ Buttons can be used to create dimension by clustering them.
♥ Buttons can be the focal point of the whole design.
♥ Buttons can be functional in a closing.
♥ Buttons can be tucked in special places.

ibbon Magic

I teach a class at my store called "Ribbon Magic" a[nd] that's exactly how I feel about ribbons. They creat[e] special magic by being just what they are – pretty, sh[iny] or textured, flowing streamers, little rosebuds, bows. Ribbons have, since V[ic-]torian days, been the crowning glory to set off a table or a garment. Old perio[di-]cals and books on antiques show the many fascinating uses of ribbons. Th[ey] were lost to us at the turn of the century, but now are finding a place in our liv[es] as we once again embellish ourselves and our surroundings. Today's ribbo[ns] are polyester and, although polyester has a mind of its own and is often hard [to] manipulate, it is completely washable. Customers and students continua[lly] ask, "What will happen when it's washed?" Nothing, I tell them, and it's tr[ue.] Here are some techniques and ideas about ribbons for you.

Ribbons can be folded like prairie points and used as an edging or as a tri[m.] To fold a prairie point, use ribbon 1" wide by 1½". Fold as indicated in drawing at right. The extra edges are stitched into the seam. You can use the flat side forward or the side that shows the ribbon edges.

Use ribbon as a straight trim. The pinafore in the center of photo **37** shows how ⅛" wide ribbons can be stitched by machine with one line of stitching. Pin the ribbon in place and then, with your left hand on the start of the fabric and your right hand on the fabric to be fed through the machine, guide the ribbon through. Satin ribbon is slippery, so this technique works well. A tiny zigzag stitch could be used, but I feel that is a "manufactured" look. A wider ribbon needs stitching on both edges. You can fuse the ribbon in place with fusible web. This works well if you choose to place several ribbons butted together. Be sure to get a good fuse. Repetition works well with ribbons. Several rows of ribbon are usually more effective than just one row. You can run into a lot of expense with ribbons, so plan your strategy.

Use ribbon as a curved trim. On the edge that will be on the inside of a curve, run a line of gathering. Pull the gathering thread to fit the curve. Stitch in place and press lightly.

Attach ribbons with embroidery stitches. (See photos 17C, 29C and 33B.) Since I love handwork, this really appeals to me. It gives me a place to use my stitchery and try out ideas. In Back to Basics, the executions of some embroidery stitches are diagrammed. Regular six-strand floss, silk or DMC pearl cotton all work well. The shinier threads show up more. You can choose a thread color the same as the ribbon or a contrasting color. French knots create little knots or circles on the ribbon. There are two ways to approach the knots. Use six strands and wrap the needle once, or use two strands and wrap two or three times. I don't like the knots too large because they catch on things. When attaching a narrow ribbon, the herringbone stitch can be used like couching, covering the whole ribbon. Feather stitches used on wider ribbons make a nice viney effect. Butttons stitched on ribbons can hold them down (see photos 29C and 33B). Old crazy quilts are full of stitching ideas and many of them can be applied to ribboned garments.

Ribbon ruffling can be used as an edging or to highlight a part of the patchwork. This can be done by hand or by machine. Choose a ribbon at least ¾" wide. The narrower ones are just too small. Stitch in diagonal lines along the ribbon. Pull it up and you will have a double ruffle. For a nice full ruffle, double the length needed.

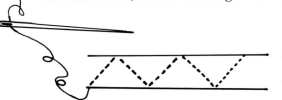

Make ribbon rosettes from a ribbon piece ¾" wide and 9" long. Fold back one raw edge. Hand or machine gather ¼" from the edge, then pull the thread until the ribbon forms a circle. Place the folded edge over the raw edge and tack it in place. A cluster of these with button centers look nice. (See photos 29C and 29E.) One alone isn't usually as effective.

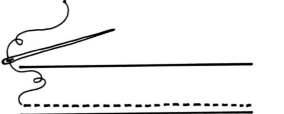

Ribbon leaves complement your flowers. Use 1" wide ribbon, ¾" long. Fold ribbon to a point, make a little tuck, then gather the wide edge so leaf is dimensional. Tack leaves under flowers.

Ribbon weaving is not a new technique, but I will share some of the points that I find make it easier. (See photo 25A.) To determine yardage, measure the space to be filled and cut a piece of fusible interfacing that size, plus ½" seam allowances. The width of the ribbons can vary, if you choose. Place them next to each other until you have enough to fill the space. Double that amount, since you need to weave across. Yardage is difficult to plan until you know the width of ribbons to be used. I usually lay them out at the store and decide.

To do the weaving, work at your ironing board. Plug in the iron and have plenty of pins handy. Place the fusible interfacing on the ironing board with the fusible side facing you. Lay enough ribbons vertically on the interfacing to cover it. Push a pin through each one to hold it in place. Next, cut ribbons the width of the interfacing. Start next to the pins and weave each ribbon through the vertical ribbons. For plain weave, you go over one and under one. For a basket weave, you go over two and under one. Once the surface is filled, press with an up and down motion, fusing the ribbons to the interfacing.

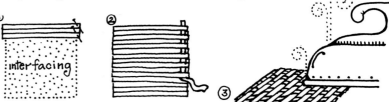

All kinds of woven designs are possible. Someday I would like to do a collar, using ⅛" wide satin ribbons. Wouldn't that be pretty? Ribbon weaving can stand alone, like a piece of lace as a medallion or to embellish other piecing.

uffles

There are all kinds of ruffles in all kinds of places. Not only garments, but pillows, bedspreads and tablecloths are good places for ruffles. Usually, a ruffle finishes an edge. It is the final statement in a composition. Here are some rules of thumb to use in calculating yardage for ruffles.

♥ Measure the distance to be ruffled and double it for a nice, full ruffle. Add even more if you desire the fullness. Purchased little girls' dresses in the low price range often don't double the fullness for ruffles, although higher priced ones use 1½ to two times the fullness. The long pastel pinafore in photo 33F has 90" in the skirt for a 22" waist, and the ruffle on the bottom of the skirt is 180" of fabric.

♥ Allow at least ½" for the top edge of the ruffle to be gathered. Allow ½" for a clean finished hem.

♥ To run a line of stitching for gathering, set the machine stitching length at 8 stitches per inch. To gather, hold the bobbin thread and push the fabric from each end to the center. If you have a long line of ruffling, lay lightweight fish line or quilting thread down and zigzag stitch across it — it pulls up so easily, you'll be surprised.

Here are some sketches of ruffle ideas.

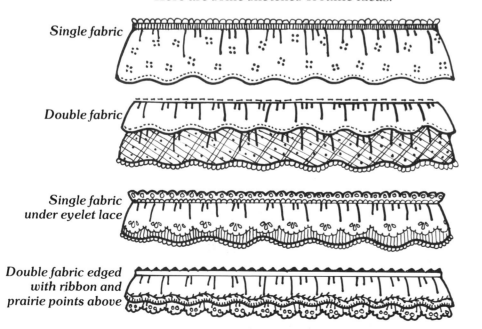

Single fabric

Double fabric

Single fabric under eyelet lace

Double fabric edged with ribbon and prairie points above

Hanky-panky

Hankies are a lot like laces in their use, so read that section if you haven't already. My grandmother always used hankies, so I remember them from my childhood. I notice them more in clothing now as a decoration. One corner is usually decorated more than the others, so it can become a yoke, a flap on a blouse pocket, a pocket design, collar or part of a crazy quilt design. You could use the straight edges as a cuff on a blouse or a border on a small section. Several hankies can be combined in piecing. The sheer batiste ones are pretty over a bright color like transparent appliqué. The ideas are endless, just put your head to work!

Dresser scarves can be used in the same way. Photo 9E shows a dresser scarf as a center of interest. Most of the design was on the end, so the grid style quilting helped balance the end with the design. Joyce Coats appliquéd a dresser scarf to the body of the jacket shown in photo 13A. It almost appears that the designs were embroidered on the jacket.

Piping

Pipings are a form of edging with a more tailored appearance. You see piping on pillows and around edges of vests and jackets. Piping can be purchased in a notions department or you can make your own. It is a strip of fabric folded over cording so it appears sculptured.

To construct your own piping, cut strips of fabric in a width to fit over the cord you have chosen. Allow for ½" seam allowances. I used to always cut my fabric on the bias, but one of my friends has been experimenting by cutting it on the straight of the grain. If there aren't many drastic curves to go around, it works and is sure easier. There are lots of cordings on the market from ⅛" to 1" wide. Make sure the cording is washable and is preshrunk before you put fabric over it.

To make the piping, put the zipper foot on the sewing machine. Fold the fabric over the cord and stitch as close to the cord as you can. Here are some ideas to try with piping . . . Do more than one row of piping, all the same width (see photos 12D, 24D, 25A and 29B) . . . Make piping different widths . . . Insert piping between rows of strip piecing . . . Make piping different widths . . . Use the unexpected fabric like satin, corduroy, velveteen or velour (see photos 25A and 29E).

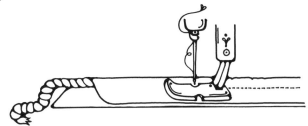

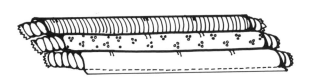

Borders

When thinking about trimming, borders come to mind. They are something extra, they draw the eye to that place on the garment. (See photo 12E and 25B.) Border prints have always been around, but I think it's nice to make your own.

Sometimes you don't want the whole garment pieced or you don't have time to piece a whole garment. At other times, a border can become a center of interest. It's easier for detailed work to stand out in a border form.

Maybe you have a limited amount of lace or trim and need a small place to use it. In the rose pink jacket with front, neck and back border (photo 25A), I had limited amounts of old lace and just four of the ceramic buttons. I also used the border as a place to try some ideas I'd been toying with, like ribbon weaving.

The only caution I would make is that the border should not overwhelm the other fabric in width or design. You may need to pipe it to distinguish it from the other fabric. You might even make a border that serves as a medallion on a vest or jacket (photo 24D).

Putting it all Together

The following are three approaches to construction of jackets and vests. I have used jackets and vests for my examples because they are the most difficult. Borders or a yoke on a dress are much easier to execute. You should have in mind some idea of the design of the garment before beginning. Each approach is more appropriate for the particular shapes described. Choose the one that makes your job easiest. By the time you finish, you will have discovered ideas of your own. Just keep in mind there's always a way!

Creative Cutups

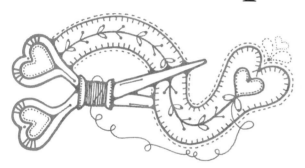

This method works well for overall patch designs that emcompass the whole garment. Many traditional blocks work well here. Basically, you stitch fabric together to fit each pattern piece. You are creating your own yardage. The more I used this method, the more creative I became. I used to find a traditional block I liked and then work with it until it fit the garment. Photo 12B shows a Kings Cross design adapted to a jacket back. I'm now becoming brave enough to draw my own patterns. This same technique of cutting up the pattern pieces was used in the jackets shown in photos 13C and 25D. The curves were not drastic enough in the latter jacket to be a problem.

Following are the basic steps:
♥ Trace the pattern pieces onto tracing paper. Be sure to include notches, grain line and any other instructions necessary for construction.
♥ Using a ruler, mark off your desired shapes.
♥ Number each space you have drawn.
♥ You may want to decide which fabric you want where and make a note of it on the space.
♥ Sketch a sample drawing of the garment pieces, including numbers and fabric identification. You will need this when you stitch it all together.

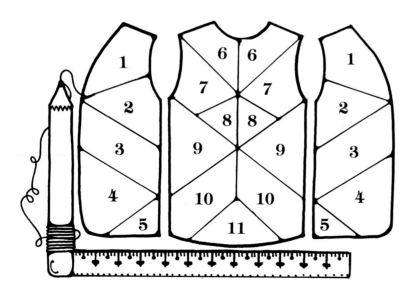

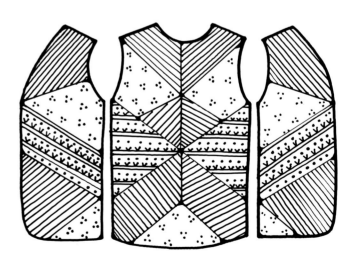

♥ Write "add seam allowance" on each side of all the lines you have drawn. You wouldn't want to forget because it won't fit together if you don't.

♥ Cut the pattern apart, stacking the pieces together that will be cut from the same fabric.

♥ Lay the pattern pieces on the fabric, leaving ¼" or ½" seam allowance around all pieces. Have the right side of the pattern facing you on all pieces. If one is flipped over, it will be upside down when you sew it together. Cut out all pieces.

♥ Before starting to sew these together, lay them all out to be sure it's what you have invisioned.

♥ Sew all the pieces together. Press all seams in one direction.

♥ Cut out the lining and padding from the original pattern. Decide if you want binding around the edges or if you want the lining to finish the edge. Essentially, this technique is like making a quilt; once you've layered it with batting and lining, quilt it by hand or by machine.

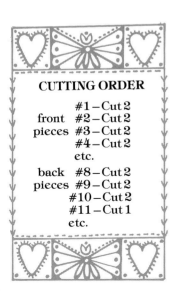

CUTTING ORDER

front pieces
#1 – Cut 2
#2 – Cut 2
#3 – Cut 2
#4 – Cut 2
etc.

back pieces
#8 – Cut 2
#9 – Cut 2
#10 – Cut 2
#11 – Cut 1
etc.

Coming Attractions: Cut-Ups combines with String Patching on Page 32.

Photo 24A. Marina Wood designed the "Fat Cat" for Jean's medallion pieced jacket.

Photo 24C. A fan-shaped doily fits perfectly on the bodice of this sundress. Tiny gathered ribbons create flowers at the end of each ribbon thread (Page 19).

Photo 24D. "My Heart's Fancy" includes two of Jean's favorite shapes, hearts and fans. The design was inspired by the gold heart buttons, a gift from a friend. Triple rows of piping define the design and emphasize the color scheme. (See Page 21).

Photo 24B. An 88¢ doily inspired this subtle-toned jacket. Pearl buttons reemphasize the doily shape. Strip pieced chintz and eyelet contribute to the elegance of the jacket design.

Photo 24E. Carrol Clark's grandmother left her several Dresden Plate quilt blocks that Carrol set into a garment for herself. The navy blue contrast sets off the pastel colors in the plates.

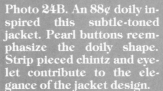

Photo 25B. This vest shows a contemporary inter-pretation of traditional hand quilting (Page 15).

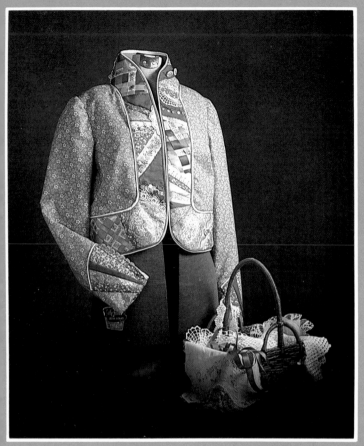

Photo 25D. Creative Cut-ups were never so bright! Simple lines traced onto a paper pattern made this vest a rainbow delight. A gold hand dangles a bun-dle of stuffed hearts from the closing.

Photo 25C. Sally Paul loves hearts and pigs. so it's only natural that she designed this patchwork (24 pieces) pig. Prairie points (Page 48) border the medallion while chevron style string patching fin-ishes off the vest back (Page 30).

Photo 25A. Ribbon weaving (Page 19), old lace and special buttons make a unique border design for a jacket of dusty rose. Double rows of satin piping separate the print and the border (see page 21). Simple fans embellish the sleeve edge.

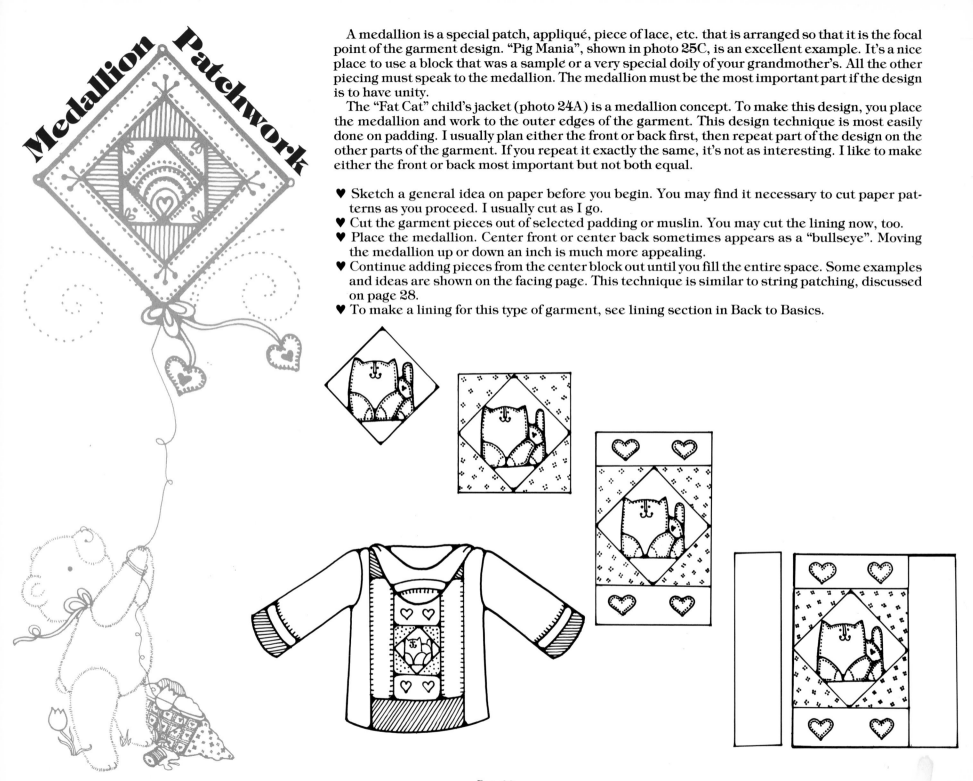

Medallion Patchwork

A medallion is a special patch, appliqué, piece of lace, etc. that is arranged so that it is the focal point of the garment design. "Pig Mania", shown in photo 25C, is an excellent example. It's a nice place to use a block that was a sample or a very special doily of your grandmother's. All the other piecing must speak to the medallion. The medallion must be the most important part if the design is to have unity.

The "Fat Cat" child's jacket (photo 24A) is a medallion concept. To make this design, you place the medallion and work to the outer edges of the garment. This design technique is most easily done on padding. I usually plan either the front or back first, then repeat part of the design on the other parts of the garment. If you repeat it exactly the same, it's not as interesting. I like to make either the front or back most important but not both equal.

♥ Sketch a general idea on paper before you begin. You may find it necessary to cut paper patterns as you proceed. I usually cut as I go.

♥ Cut the garment pieces out of selected padding or muslin. You may cut the lining now, too.

♥ Place the medallion. Center front or center back sometimes appears as a "bullseye". Moving the medallion up or down an inch is much more appealing.

♥ Continue adding pieces from the center block out until you fill the entire space. Some examples and ideas are shown on the facing page. This technique is similar to string patching, discussed on page 28.

♥ To make a lining for this type of garment, see lining section in Back to Basics.

String Patching

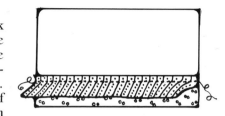
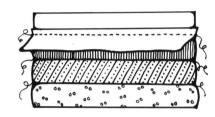

String patching or quick quilting is a very old from of patchwork and very easy, too! I think it developed when fabric was very scarce and our ancestors found it necessary to use narrow scrap pieces of fabric. I like the freedom this form of piecing allows. You can approach it where each strip is measured and cut exactly (photo 33D), or you can cut strips of various widths (photo 17B). I like to use varying widths and make decisions as I go. I think there is a richness of feeling that comes from blending fabrics together. Let me explain guide you through a small project to help you understand string piecing.

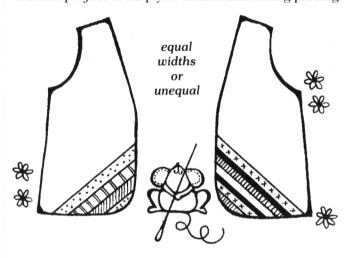

equal widths or unequal

Cut a square of muslin or padding about 4" square. Cut strips of fabric varying widths (½", ¾", 1"). Place the first fabric right side up on the bottom of the square even with the raw edge. Place the right side of the second strip on the right side of the first strip. Machine stitch through all three layers, ¼" in the same way from the raw edges. Turn the second strip right side up and add another, then another. You can achieve a thinner strip by taking a larger seam allowance.

♥ Cut the garment pattern pieces from needlepunch, thermolam, muslin or flannel. You need a stable surface to stitch through. Sheet batting alone moves around too much. It can be used with a muslin piece, but will be thicker.

♥ Cut your strips. Different looks can be achieved by how the strips are cut. Wide strips all the identical width appear formal. Strips cut varying widths ½" to 1½" appear to have a molded appearance. They blend together like you have created your own piece of yardage. Strips with a variety of texture (like broadcloth with corduroy or velveteen) appear richer.

♥ Now decide the angle at which you will sew. Horizontal will give a feeling of width (the eye moves back and forth). Vertical gives a feeling of height. Right angle and chevron will appear more slimming. Combine the angles to achieve a string patch, crazy quilt feeling. Draw a simple sketch of what you want the garment to look like. I sometimes draw a line on the needlepunch to indicate the angle I intend to work.

♥ Once you finish the string piecing, sew the garment together and line it as described in Back to Basics.

The following pages offer examples and actual instructions for some string patch variations.

Photo 28. Jean cut pillow case edging lace to decorate the string piecing in this pretty blue vest.

Photo 29E. Fans are pieced together and turned upside down to create a continuous border around the bottom of this jacket. The fan strips are embellished with ribbons, laces and fancy embroidery stitches. Buttons add the final touch as they serpentine the bottom of the border.

Photo 29A. Fred Wells calls this the "gingerbread" jacket. It is Jean's country provincial interpretation.

Photo 29B. Strip piecing creates a vertical border on the front of this jacket, made by Marina Wood for her mother. Channel machine quilting emphasizes the vertical effect.

Photo 29C. Fans step into the picture as a pinafore bib, decorated with buttons and gathered ribbon flowers (see Pages 18, 19). Note the fan shapes in the lace trim.

CHEVRON STYLE

To achieve a chevron stripe, start with a triangle. The height and width of the triangle dictate the shape of the chevron – a low long triangle produces a subtle chevron. (See photo 33D).

♥ Place the triangle where you want the chevron to start. You might cut out a yoke on a shirt with a "V" and let the "V" be your triangle.

♥ Stitch a strip to one side, then the other, trimming each strip after you turn the fabric up. For a more informal look, stitch two or three strips to one side then a different amount to the other side. It's usually helpful to pencil a line from the point of the triangle up to the top to maintain an even center.

STRING PATCH SECTIONS

♥ Divide the pattern into four sections. Add seam allowances where you cut it apart.
♥ Start with identical triangles in each section. Continue piecing outward until all sections are filled in.

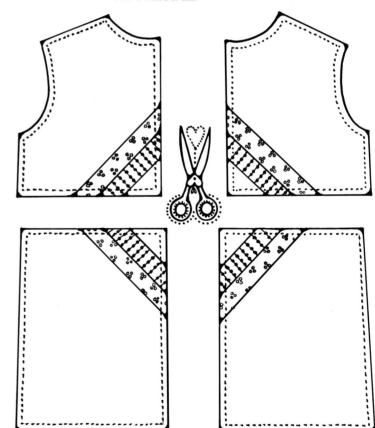

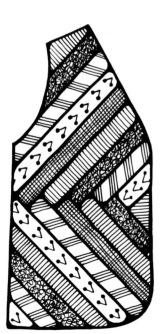
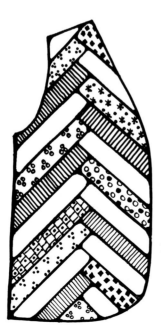
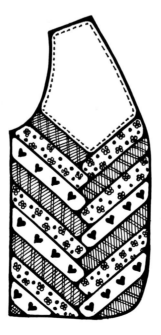

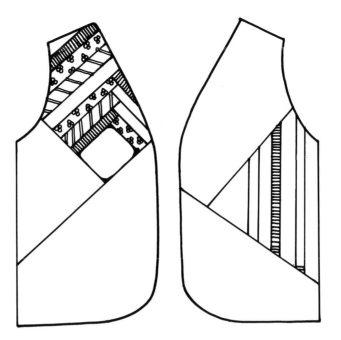

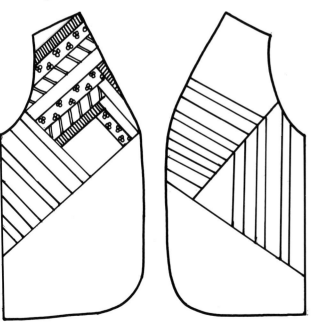

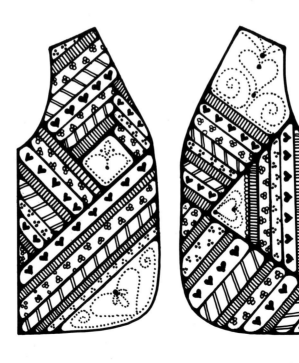

Numbers indicate order in which strips should be sewn, arrows indicate direction of strips.

CRAZY STRING

Divide each pattern piece of the garment into sections. Usually, three is plenty. Be sure to put an arrow in each section to indicate the direction in which the strips will be pieced. In some sections, you may want to insert an interesting piece of lace or quilt a design on a solid piece of fabric. This acts as a medallion or center of interest in each section. If you choose this technique, place these pieces on the foundation first.

Look closely at the arrows you have indicated on each section. Plan the strip piecing so that the first strip in each new section will cover the raw edges of the last section you pieced. If you goof, you can always hand stitch a strip in place.

CUT-UP SHAPES

I use this for shirt yokes, like the one in photo 33A.

♥ Stitch together strips until you have a piece of fabric up to 12" wide and 45" long. Press all seam allowances in one direction.

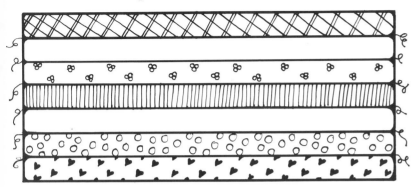

♥ Draw your yoke section on paper. Divide it up like you do in "Creative Cut-ups". Put an arrow in each section, indicating the direction the strips should take.

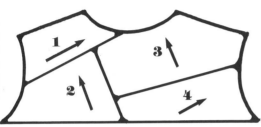

♥ Cut paper apart and place sections on the strips with arrows all going in the same direction. Leave room between pieces to add a ¼" seam allowance. Cut out all the pattern pieces.

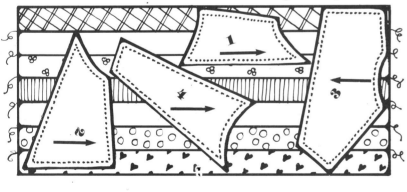

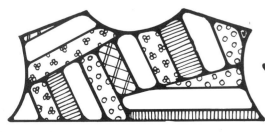

♥ Stitch all the sections back together.

STRING PATCHED STRIPS

♥ Stitch several strips of fabric together, varying the widths of the strips. Press all seam allowances in one direction.

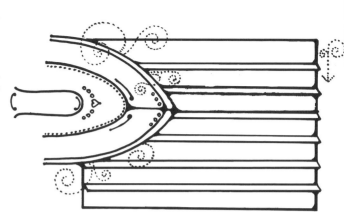

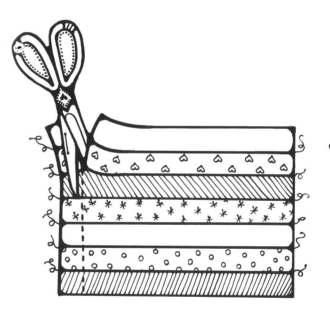

♥ Cut across the strips, making them at least 1½" wide. These can be stitched into one long strip.

♥ Use them as a border by adding fabric to each side of the patchwork. (See photo 29A.)

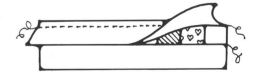

Photo 33A. Strip piecing cut into shapes and stitched back together forms the yoke of Jason's shirt.

Photo 33D. Chevron string piecing lends a slenderizing angle to patchwork (see Page 30). Hand quilted flowers dominate the triangle that sets the angle for the piecing.

Photo 33C. String piecing is often used to finish off a medallion design like this. Jean used only part of a doily for the medallion because the whole piece was too large. This technique can salvage a damaged lace or doily.

Photo 33E. Carrol Clark made a pieced basket into this dress yoke.

Photo 33F. Transparent appliqué creates a muted effect over the hearts in this skirt border (Page 15). Note the use of pastel fabrics and ribbons embroidered in place. Lace tops the border and a ribbon trimmed fabric ruffle finishes the bottom.

Photo 33B. Voile makes a soft, transparent layer over the ribbons and trims of this dress yoke. Brazilian embroidery was worked on the ribbons.

Beginnings for your very own Paper Dolls

Most of us went through the paper doll stage as little girls. I used to sit and dream up new outfits, cutting and pasting and coloring along the way. My mother saved some of the early doll clothes I made; I was rather inventive, but not very skilled with the needle. Children's clothing is my favorite form of sewing. Part of it is the fantasy of creating something for a special little person. I've always found children's clothes great to try ideas without getting into a huge project. I can put all those ruffles and frills on a little girl that I'm not comfortable wearing myself. I think it's very important that garments reflect a child's personality.

Before starting a child's project, really exercise your imagination. Look for ideas in coloring books, newspapers, greeting cards, wrapping paper. Remember, one idea leads to another. Clip and save anything that catches your eye. Think about color. Children can wear dynamic color combinations and unexpected colors, too. Some of the prettiest little girl dresses today are brown, navy or burgundy, highlighted with beautiful ribbons and laces.

My daughter has been coming to the store since she was four, being around people making choices. One day when she was six, she wanted to look in the pattern book like the customers, choose a pattern and fabric. I got busy and wasn't paying much attention. Here she came with a pattern (the right size, too) and three well coordinated cotton prints that she had chosen herself. She then proceeded to show me how each would be used. I was so surprised! She tuned in to what people were doing at the store, and it taught me an important lesson — children do have some very good ideas and, with limited guidance, can make some choices. Why not let your little person help on the garment? You might make a wide range selection to let them choose from if that makes you feel more comfortable.

In this part of the book, I will offer you some plans for working up actual garments without buying a pattern. I will also cover working with commercial patterns. Pay close attention to Marina's illustrations.

Working with Patterns

Commercial patterns keep going up in price, just like everything else, and children do grow. So, here are some ideas to help you make more use of your patterns.

♥ Sizing from one size to another usually means adding ¼" to each side and shoulder seam. On a sleeve, add ¼" to each side of the seam and taper the cap of the sleeve up ¼". Add needed length. If you need to go up or down more than one size, it is more difficult.

♥ To change a basic A-line dress pattern, always remember to add a seam allowance to each side of any cut you make in a pattern. The illustrations will give you ideas. Look at ready-to-wear for more ideas.

♥ Gathered skirts are usually 45" in width, but if you want more fullness, add it. (See photo 12A.) I like to use 60" for short skirts and 80" to 90" for long ones.

♥ A basic sleeve pattern can be split and spread apart if a fuller sleeve is wanted. To make the cap fuller, add 1" at the top and taper it off to the sides. Of course, length is easily changed. To finish the bottom edge with other than a hem, you might have an elastic closing or a cuff.

♥ Pants are hard to adjust because of the crotch curve so, when I find a pair that fits, I just stick with them.

Now that you are aware of some of the possibilities in working with a basic pattern, make a trip to a children's store and see what the manufacturers have done. Then put your imagination to work!

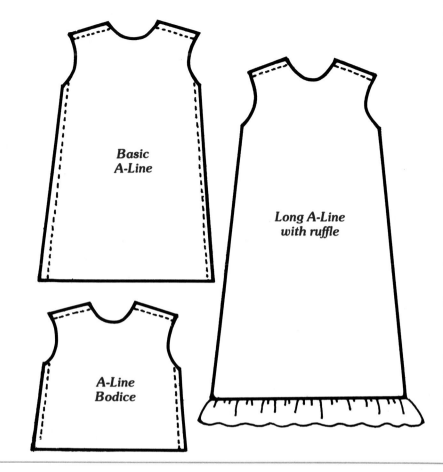

Basic A-Line

Long A-Line with ruffle

A-Line Bodice

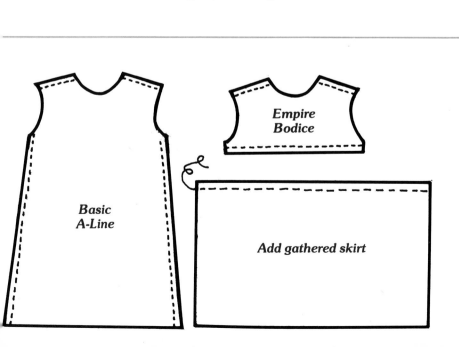

Basic A-Line

Empire Bodice

Add gathered skirt

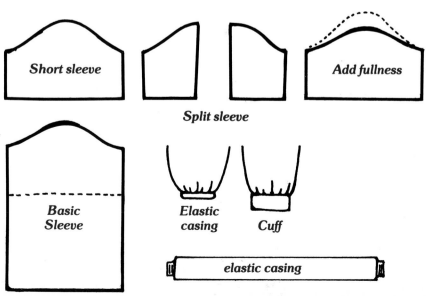

Short sleeve

Add fullness

Split sleeve

Basic Sleeve

Elastic casing

Cuff

elastic casing

Photo 36. Panels of simple appliqué shapes form the front of the jacket at left. Its matching dirndl skirt (see p. 40) has an appliquéd heart waistband. A string patched vest like the one at center can go anywhere — with jeans or over this pretty ruffled dirndl. Little stuffed hearts dangle from a belt of coordinating ribbons. String patch shapes form the bib and pockets of the pinafore jumper at right. Double rows of eyelet give definition to the hearts, while triple rows of narrow satin ribbon trim the skirt, waistband and shoulder straps.

Photo 36A. Three-dimensional hearts (Page 15) are permanently stitched to this pinafore. The dress was worn and washed for two years before this picture was taken, so you know these free-form padded shapes really work! The color choice and offset pockets create special interest.

Photo 37. Heart shaped balloons are machine stitched to the pinafore at left (see page 41). String patching in rainbow colors emphasizes the theme of the dress. A simple jumper can be as fanciful as the pinafore shown at center, with a machine appliquéd house for a bib, trimmed with pretty lace and ribbon. Stephanie Layton made the "Sweetheart Vest" designed by Marina Wood, shown at right. The heart shaped flowers are decorative and functional as a front closing. The simple ruffled dirndl skirt completes the outfit.

Photos 37A, 37B. Ribbon magic works wonders on simple pinafore jumpers, transforming a simple dress into unique garments for special little people.

Measurements

Children are constantly growing and changing shape, so take measurements often. You might want to keep a card in your purse with your child's measurements so you can have them when you go shopping. Any measurements we give are the average used in commercial pattern books. You might make your child a chart like the one below and then you can both see how and where they are growing. Always measure over undergarments and pull the measuring tape to a comfortable snugness. Children's clothes should allow them room to grow or to accommodate sweaters and other heavy undergarments. After each measurement, I've included the average ease needed. Add that to your child's measurements. This is what your pattern should measure — child's measurement + ease.

Child's name: _____   **Age:** _____

	Measurement	Ease	Measurement plus Ease
Chest	_____	2"	_____
Waist	_____	¾" to 1"	_____
Hips	_____	2" to 3"	_____
Sleeve Length	_____	1"	_____
Backwaist (base of neck to waist)	_____	¾" to 1"	_____
Skirt Length (no ease needed)	Short____ Midcalf____ Long____		

AVERAGE MEASUREMENTS

When you are shopping for fabric, it is helpful to know the average measurements of a child at a particular age. If you need a skirt length, for example, you can readily judge what you need from this chart. If you are sewing for someone you are unable to measure, this is a reasonable guide.

	Size 4	Size 6	Size 8	Size 10	Size 12
Chest	23"	25"	27"	28½"	30"
Waist	21"	22"	23½"	24½"	25"
Hip	24"	26"	28"	30"	32"
Approximate Height	41"	47"	52"	56"	58"
Dress Length	20"	24"	27"	29"	31"

Making a Pattern

You may find it necessary to make your own patterns. Many fabric stores carry a thin, non-woven fabric for making patterns that is nice to work on and doesn't tear. Or, choose brown wrapping paper or newspaper.

For each design, measurements are given for each size. These do not include seam allowance. Remember to <u>add seam allowances</u>! Most commercial patterns allow ⅝". You can use ½" if it's easier. You may want to dot in your seam allowance in a contrasting color on your paper pattern. Nearly all patterns use squares or rectangles so patterns aren't always necessary. It just depends on how you like to work.

The following symbols help me to remember what I'm doing. I mark these on my paper pattern as I make it.

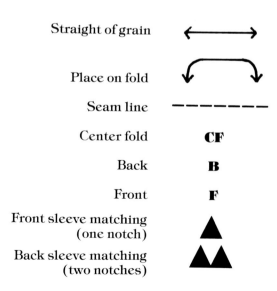

AVERAGE YARDAGE REQUIREMENTS

	Size 4	Size 6	Size 8	Size 10	Size 12
Plain Dirndl Skirt	¾ yd	1 yd	1¼ yd	1¼ yd	1⅜ yd
Dirndl Skirt	½ yd	¾ yd	1 yd	1 yd	1 yd
Coordinating Ruffle	¼ yd	¼ yd	¼ yd	¼ yd	¼ yd
Short Pinafore Jumper	1 yd	1¼ yd	1½ yd	1½ yd	1⅝ yd
Long Pinafore Jumper	1¼ yd	1½ yd	1¾ yd	1¾ yd	2 yd
5" Pinafore Ruffle	⅓ yd	⅓ yd	⅓ yd	⅓ yd	⅓ yd
Long Sleeved Jacket	1¼ yd	1¼ yd	1½ yd	1½ yd	1¾ yd
Vest	½ yd	⅝ yd	⅝ yd	⅝ yd	¾ yd

Straight of grain	⟷
Place on fold	⤵⤵
Seam line	– – – – – –
Center fold	**CF**
Back	**B**
Front	**F**
Front sleeve matching (one notch)	▲
Back sleeve matching (two notches)	▲▲

Dirndl Skirt

The dirndl skirt has been popular for years and is an especially wearable child's garment. This skirt has an elastic casing for growing room and a ruffled skirt. If the girl happens to grow a lot suddenly, you can just add a longer ruffle! This skirt is so simple that my beginner children's sewing class makes them. Top it with a pretty blouse or turtleneck and vest and you have a great, changeable outfit! (See photos 36 and 37).

Measurements needed:

		Total
Waist_____	Cut elastic exact waist measurement	
Waist to ruffle_____	Add 3"	_____
Ruffle_____	Double skirt width and add 1"	_____

Average yardage requirements are given on Page 39. A ¼ yard of fabric is enough for a contrasting ruffle. You will need ⅜" wide elastic cut to the child's waist size. Optional trims will require up to 1¼ yard of lace and/or ribbon. I don't make paper patterns for this project; I just measure directly on the fabric.

♥ Sew the center back seam, using a ½" seam allowance. Press seam open.

♥ At the ironing board, press the top edge of the skirt back 2½".

♥ Along the top edge, stitch 1" from the fold sewing through both thicknesses.

SKIRT

♥ Overlap ends of the elastic ½"; stitch the ends together.

♥ Place the circle of elastic between the skirt fabric and casing. Turn under the raw edge of the casing and top stitch it to the skirt, encasing the elastic as you go. The top of the skirt will gather along the elastic. **Note:** Another method for making a gathered waist like this is to finish the casing and then, opening the center seam between the casing stitching lines, thread the elastic through the casing. Join the ends of the elastic as described.

♥ Seam the ruffle pieces end to end with a ½" seam allowance. Press seam open.

♥ Machine hem the bottom of the ruffle by turning under ¼" and then another ¼". Press, then machine top stitch. This is a clean finished edge.

♥ Run a line of gathering stitches ½" from the raw top edge of the ruffle. If you're having trouble gathering, use dual duty thread or lay fish line on the stitching line and loosely zigzag over it, then pull up the fish line. Many people find it easier to stitch two basting lines, one ¼" from the edge, the other ½" from the edge. This gives you two bobbin threads to gather.

♥ Pull gathers until ruffle fits the bottom edge of the skirt. Pin ruffle to skirt, matching right sides and raw edges. If you are adding an extra lace ruffle, place lace between the two layers. Stitch a ½" seam. Sometimes I use a wide zigzag stitch to finish the raw edges.

♥ If ribbon trim is desired above the ruffle, top stitch ribbon through the skirt fabric only. Stitching through seam allowances is too bulky.

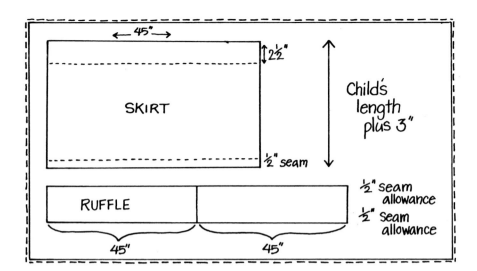

← 45" →

SKIRT

2½"

½" seam

Child's length plus 3"

RUFFLE

½" seam allowance

½" seam allowance

45"

45"

Pinafore Jumper

The pinafore jumper is an easy way to try all kinds of small projects on the bibs. By looking at the photographs, you will see all kinds of shapes derived from the basic bib. The skirt length can change for the occasion, too. Or, put a bib on a pair of pants. Little boys wear overalls, so here's a place to sew for the boys. You can also make the pinafore with only a front waistband and skirt to make it an apron. Make an apron for grandma or to wear over a pretty dress (photos 12E and 25G). When I make an apron, I put a loop at each end of the waistband and the ties come over the shoulders, cross and hook through the waistband loop to tie in the center back. The same formula works for ladies' aprons.

Measurements needed:
Waist _____   Skirt Length _____
Length from back waist,
    over shoulder to front waist _____

If ruffles are desired, refer to the dirndl skirt section. Average yardage requirements are on Page 38. You will also need a 7" skirt zipper and ¼ yard of interfacing for the waistband. Other trims depend on the theme chosen.

♥ For the bib, you need a 10" square for adults and children size 12. For sizes 4-6, cut an 8" square; sizes 8-10 need a 9" square. Make one bib front and cut another piece the same size for a facing. Cut two waistband pieces, 2½" wide and as long as the waist measurement plus 2". Cut two strap pieces, 2½" wide and as long as the over-the-shoulder measurement plus 2". For the skirt, cut a 45" wide piece as long as the desired skirt length plus 3". I sometimes use a double fullness (90" instead of 45") for dressy garments. Accommodations for ruffles are given in the dirndl skirt directions.

♥ Do any desired patchwork or appliqué on the bib and skirt before stitching any pieces together. Add piping to edges if desired.

♥ Right sides together, stitch ½" seams along the long edge and one end of each strap; trim corners. Press seams open. Turn right side out and press again.

♥ Pin the raw edge of the straps at the top corners of the bib. Place bib lining to bib front, matching right sides. Stitch the top and sides ½" from the edge. Trim curves and corners, if necessary. Turn to right side and press.

♥ Find center front of waistband; mark it with a pin. Center the bib on the waistband. Pin,

matching right sides and raw edges. Place the waistband facing on top of the bib piece so that the right sides and raw edges of the waistband pieces are matching. Stitch ½" from the edge and sides of the waistband. Trim corners, then turn to right side.

♥ Run a line of gathering stitches ½" from the edge of the skirt. Gather top edge until it fits waistband.

♥ Seam the center back of the skirt within 7" of the top edge. Put zipper in. Pin skirt to waistband, right sides together. Sew ½" from the top edge. Turn waistband to right side. Press under the raw edges of the waistband lining and hand or machine top stitch it in place.

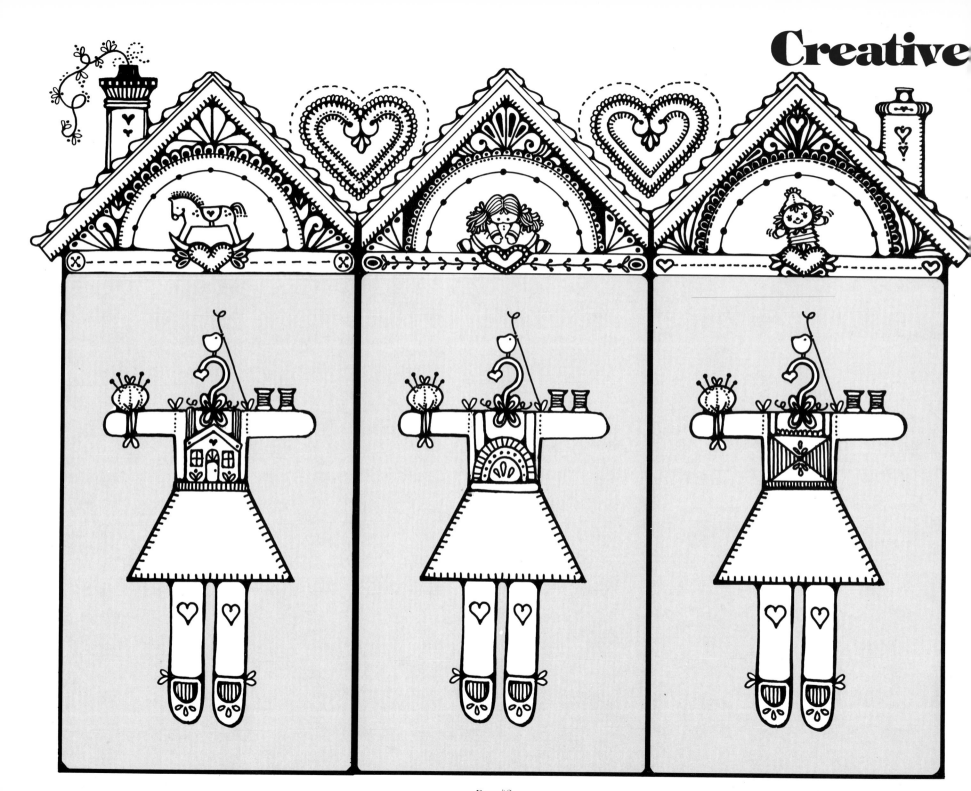

Bibworks!

Jackets & Vests for Children

Jackets and vests are discussed in detail in Putting it all Together. The Theme section will give you ideas, too. Since you want the child to wear what you make, the decorating should be durable (machine stitched) and the garment comfortable. Sleeves sometimes need to be made larger because the padding takes up space. Pull the pattern around the arm of the child and be sure you have 2" extra – 1" is be taken up by the pad. A raglan sleeve is great.

Children like jeans, so vests are nice toppers. Then, make a skirt or dress the vest can be worn with, too. Vests really have lots of uses and they are warm. Usually, you will want to put buttons and buttonholes or ties on a child's vest to keep it in place. This is a place you might work in special buttons. Photo 12A shows a vest that was designed just for the kitty buttons my daughter discovered one day. On this page are ideas for children's vests and jackets.

Reverse appliqué butterfly

Just thinking of all those fun patching projects

Ice cream cone is a real pocket

"Yum Yum"

Barnyard Patches

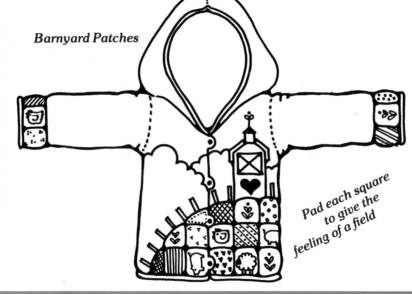

Pad each square to give the feeling of a field

Background might be string patched or striped fabric

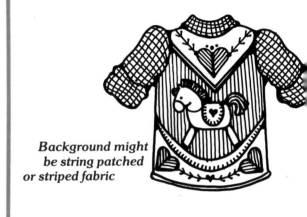

"Good Morning, Sunshine"

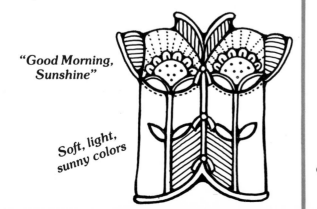

Soft, light, sunny colors

"Clowning Around"

Real fabric ruffle at clown's neck

Rainbow might be bias tape. . .for a boy, leave off ruffles.

Have a rainbow day!

*Balloons form closing
on vest – pad them and
put snaps behind*

School Days!

*Use a real bell
for the schoolhouse*

*Ruffle my skirt;
tie me up with
tiny ribbons*

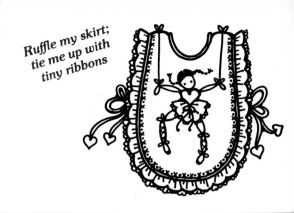

*Buttonhole stitch
decorates piecing*

Choo-Choo Jacket

*strip sleeves
in bright solids*

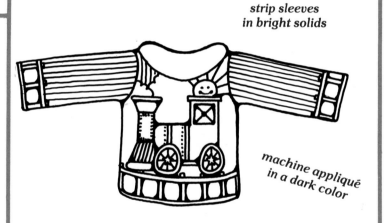

*machine appliqué
in a dark color*

"Heartbeats"

*Hearts are
little pillows,
tacked in place*

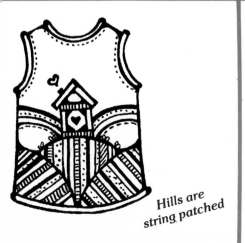

*Hills are
string patched*

*Basket is
woven ribbons*

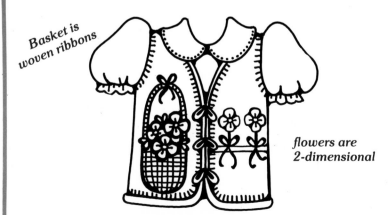

*flowers are
2-dimensional*

*Sew
Elementary*

Back

to

Basics

This is a glossary of "how-to's" mentioned earlier in the book. These are basic and to the point; for more detailed instructions, refer to more technical sewing books.

CLOSINGS

Many possibilities exist for closing a jacket or vest. Traditional buttons and buttonholes are always appropriate. Sometimes I cover a button with fabric featuring a flower in the center.

- ♥ For ties, try bias tape, ribbons or cording.
- ♥ Button loops must be made of bias to curve.
- ♥ Frogs are generally available in basic colors. Some sewing books show how to make your own.
- ♥ Discover the world of buttons in second hand and antique stores, or check the button racks at your sewing store. Some companies are making fantastic buttons now.

CLEAN FINISHED EDGE

This is a machine stitched hem. Fold under a raw edge ⅛" to ¼", then fold again. Top stitch through all layers.

CONTINUOUS BIAS BINDING

Begin by cutting two 9" squares of fabric. With a ruler, draw a diagonal line on each piece from one corner to the opposite corner (A). Cut on this line. Arrange triangles as shown in B.

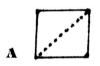

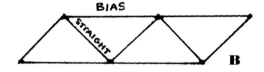

Using a ruler, mark off 1½" sections (C).

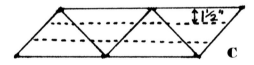

Bring the ends of the piece together, matching right sides. Instead of matching line A with line A, however, match A with B, offsetting one row. Sew a ¼" seam. Press seam open. Begin cutting at A and cut around and around until you have one long strip of bias binding.

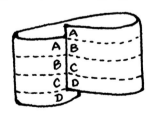

EMBROIDERY STITCHES

French knot

Feather

Chain

Buttonhole

Herringbone

Cross Stitch

Stem Stitch

LINING JACKETS & VESTS

You have two choices of lining techniques. A garment can have a binding around the edge or it can be plain. Jackets and vests are both finished the same if binding is used. The shoulder and side seams are sewn and pressed open on the outer fabric and the lining fabric. Sleeves are set in jackets. Place the wrong side of the

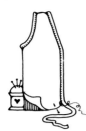

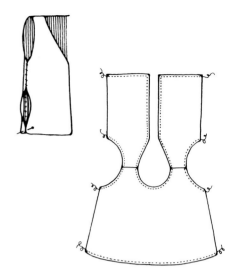

lining to the wrong side of the garment and pin all edges. Cut bias binding (see opposite page) to fit edges. Pin binding on outside of garment and stitch ¼" from the edge. Turn bias to the wrong side, turning under the edge. Machine or hand stitch it in place on the lining side. Commercial extra wide double fold bias tape or French fold bias tape can be used instead of home-made binding.

To line a plain jacket, begin by stitching all the seams in the jacket and the lining. Press all seams open. Place right side of lining next to right side of jacket and pin in place. Start stitching at the center back and continue around the jacket until you are within 6" of where you started. This 6" section is left open to turn the garment to the right side. Clip seam allowances at curves. Trim seams at corners, then turn through the 6" slot. Press all outer edges. Hand stitch the opening shut. To finish sleeves, fold in seam allowances and hand stitch in place.

There are many ways to line a plain vest and I will give you the one I use most often. You might check through commercial patterns for more ideas. Stitch the shoulder seams of the vest and the lining. Place right side of lining to right side of vest. Beginning at one side, stitch bottom of vest, up the front edges, around the neckline, across the back bottom edge and around the armholes. Clip curves and trim the corners of the seam allowances. Pull the vest through one of the side seams. Press edges and shoulder seams. Place outside of vest underarm seams together, matching at armhole and bottom edge. Stitch a ⅝" seam continu-

ing into the lining at least 1". Hand sew the rest of the lining seam. Press. Some people find it easier to press this seam allowance back before stitching to facilitate a good press when seamed.

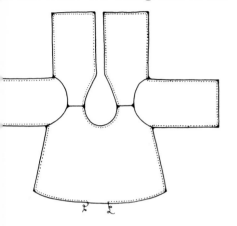

YARDAGE REQUIREMENTS FOR LADIES

Sometimes it is difficult to know just how much fabric to buy for a garment. If you need a total of 2 yards and you have chosen 4 prints, divide 4 into 2 yards and you get ½ yard. This will probably work. You can also choose to purchase ½ yard of two, ¼ yard of an accent and ¾ yard of your favorite fabric.

Many times, I buy the length of a sleeve or skirt. You can always make this work since you are piecing. If you really like one, buy a little more. The chart at right shows some average amounts for adult garments. A similar chart appears in the children's section.

In addition to fabrics, your project may also require padding, lining, notions, a zipper, thread, buttons, laces or other trims and bias tape or piping.

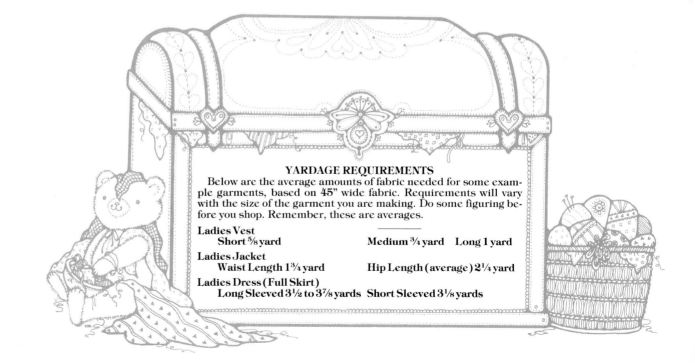

YARDAGE REQUIREMENTS
Below are the average amounts of fabric needed for some example garments, based on 45" wide fabric. Requirements will vary with the size of the garment you are making. Do some figuring before you shop. Remember, these are averages.

Ladies Vest
Short ⅝ yard   Medium ¾ yard   Long 1 yard
Ladies Jacket
Waist Length 1¾ yard   Hip Length (average) 2¼ yard
Ladies Dress (Full Skirt)
Long Sleeved 3½ to 3⅞ yards   Short Sleeved 3⅛ yards

Running Stitch

Machine Appliqué

Hand Appliqué

Blind Hem

Buttonhole Stitch

Reverse Appliqué

PADDINGS

Most jackets have some padding so they appea[r] quilted. Often the patches are stitched right to th[e] padding as in string patch. The thinnest pad is ou[t]ing flannel. It is soft and lightweight. Next in thick[]ness is 3 oz. needlepunch or fleece. This is my fa[]vorite because it is stable and less bulky than mos[t] other pads. Regular quilt batting can be used. It i[s] lofty and sculptured looking. By using a 5 oz. bat[t] you have a regular outerwear garment than can b[e] used in freezing weather. If using batting, it shoul[d] be used like you would in a quilt — piece the top an[d] place the batt between the top and the lining, the[n] machine or hand quilt. The type of padding yo[u] choose dictates the type of piecing you can do. Thi[s] is covered in the construction section of the book.

PRAIRIE POINTS

Your first time, try this technique on paper.

Take a square piece of paper at least 4" square[.] Fold it into a triangle diagonally like a bandana[.] Then, fold each end to the center. When puttin[g] prairie points on a garment, try several sizes unti[l] you have a size you like. They can be overlapped like rickrack, too. When sewn into the seam, jus[t] the folded edges are exposed. Photos 13D and 25[C] show the use of prairie points on vests.

SEW IT with HEART